DIGITAL DYNAMO: UNLEASHING YOUR MILLIONAIRE MINDSET IN THE DIGITAL AGE.

Contents

4

Introduction:

Discovering the Path to Advanced Wealth Welcoming the advanced age, where numerous opportunities abound and fortunes are readily available, In the immense scene of the web, there lies a scope of expected results for those with the vision, strength, and data to investigate it. This guide, "Computerized Tycoon Privileged insights," is your passport to advanced prosperity and success.

The world has gone through a significant change throughout recent a very long time because of the constant headway of innovation. Individuals all around the world are associated in manners that were already unfathomable thanks to the ascent of the web and cell phones. This modernized turmoil has not quite recently changed how we pass and get on to information yet has moreover prepared for one more time of undertaking and overflow creation.

In this novel scene, traditional limits to area have deteriorated, and the capacity to shape one's fate has moved heavily influenced by individuals who attempt to clutch it. The advanced world is presently open to everybody; It's like a jungle gym where anyone can build their own domain with the right mindset and strategies.

The Promise of Digital Entrepreneurship Understanding the promise of digital entrepreneurship is critical as we approach the brink of innumerable digital opportunities. The web isn't just an instrument for correspondence or a wellspring of redirection; it is a colossal business community where considerations can be changed into useful undertakings. Whether you try to start a web business store, ship off a mechanized organization, or become a substance producer, the streets for progress are unique and plentiful.

Why look into Advanced Mogul Mysteries?

You may be considering what recognizes this manual from the plenty of advanced assets. The reaction lies in base on uncovering the secrets drive individuals to advance as well concerning the area of modernized big shots. This guide goes past the basics, plunging into the viewpoint, techniques, and significant advances that can change your modernized dreams into this present reality.

The Tycoon Attitude Before we get into the practical aspects of building a computerized domain, it is essential to understand the foundation upon which success is built—the tycoon mentality. Result in the electronic scene isn't just about the latest exhibiting designs or mechanical turns of events; about fostering a mindset embraces challenges, gains from frustrations, and continually seeks after significance.

We'll take a gander at fruitful computerized business people's thought process, how they handle chance, and how they see disappointment as a chance for development as opposed to a mishap. The modernized tycoon mindset is connected to breaking freed from limiting convictions, envisioning potential results where others see impediments, and embracing a standpoint of flood.

Step by step instructions to Travel

Through the Advanced Scene The computerized scene can be both exciting and overpowering simultaneously. From virtual diversion stages and web business focuses to the intricacies of electronic exhibiting, there's a huge region to examine. In the segments ahead, we'll investigate this scene together, outfitting you with a manual for progress. You'll learn how to identify useful specialties, build a robust online presence, and use the power of online entertainment to reinforce your message.

Methods for Adaptation and Freedom from the Rat Race In today's world, wealth is more than just money; it's about commonsense and improved income sources. We'll plunge into various transformation systems, examining the universe of repeating, mechanized income, clever endeavors, and overflow defending. The goal isn't just money related accomplishment yet achieving certifiable freedom from a futile daily existence — a state where your money works for you, offering you the chance to continue with life in view of your circumstances.

Computerization, Scaling, and the Destiny of Undertaking

In the rapidly progressing automated scene, adaptability is basic. We'll examine how computerization can streamline your assignments, saving time for indispensable thinking and innovativeness. Scaling your business isn't just about advancement; about creating frameworks allows your influence to significantly expand. We will discuss emerging patterns and advancements that have the potential to influence the subsequent influx of computerized business as we look into the future.

Acquiring from the Specialists

All through this manual, you'll encounter genuine models and logical examinations of modernized investors who have arranged before you. By taking apart their journeys, triumphs, and troubles, you'll assemble huge encounters that can enlighten your own particular manner to automated wealth.

Conclusion: You're Interaction Starts

As you leave on this outing through the pages of "Cutting edge Big shot Advantaged bits of knowledge," remember that the capacity to change your automated desires into reality exists in you. This guide is most certainly not a straightforward collection of tips and tricks anyway a broad aide that, when joined with responsibility and action, can lead you to the sought after space of modernized magnates.

Could it be said that you are ready to solve the mysteries, accept the world as it is, and plot a course to digital riches? The adventure begins right now. We should change the page and enter the vast potential outcomes universe.

Getting a handle on the Modernized Scene:

Investigating the Region of Automated Open entryways

In the massive spread of the automated scene, important entryways spread out like a sweeping viewpoint fit to be examined. Understanding the complexities of this unique domain is the most important move toward computerized achievement. "Understanding the Digital Landscape" is more than just a chapter in our guidebook; the compass centers you in the right heading, helping you with disentangling the creating designs, loosen up the catch of possible results, and position yourself for thriving.

The Progression of Electronic Overflow

The high level distress has changed the principles of overflow creation, obliterating ordinary blocks and presenting a period where improvement and accessibility rule. Understanding the improvement of cutting edge overflow is critical for handle the setting of our continuous entryways. From the start of the web to the improvement of online diversion and the duplication of web business, each stage has added to a scene spilling over with potential.

As we consider this turn of events, clearly the modernized scene isn't static; it's a straightforward substance formed by mechanical types of progress, client approaches to acting, and spearheading imagination. By understanding this progression, you gain information into the examples that have formed productive undertakings and surmise those that will shape what the future holds.

Most recent things in Automated Undertaking

The electronic scene is certainly not a strong component; It is a kaleidoscope of trends, each of which presents its own unique set of opportunities for those who are able to identify and take advantage of them. Keeping up with the most recent developments is essential for anyone interested in the advanced business scene, whether they are the rise of remote work, the widespread use of e-learning, the growing significance of maintainability, or the explosion of computer-based entertainment.

In this part, we'll explore the examples that are reshaping the automated economy. Whether you're thinking about one more endeavor or hoping to improve an ongoing one, understanding these examples will give you a high ground. From the gathering of block chain advancement to the nuances of stalwart publicizing, we'll dive into the powers that are driving advancement in the automated space.

Open entryways in the Automated Economy

The electronic economy is a huge natural framework where open entryways thrive for those with the vision to clutch them. The scope of chances is broad, going from sole owners working internet based stores to global partnerships using computerized reasoning. This piece of the assistant is your fortune map, guiding you to the potential abundance hid inside the high level economy.

We'll research the various streets for cutting edge undertaking, from online business and auxiliary elevating to programming improvement and electronic organizations. If you have any desire to hang out in the computerized scene, it's critical to know the particular ventures and specialties that line up with your inclinations and abilities. Through context oriented examinations and practical pieces of information, we'll edify the pathways to advance in various high level undertakings.

The Intersection point of Advancement and Impact

At the center of the modernized scene lies the intersection point of progression and impact. Successful mechanized business visionaries are not just example fans; they are pioneers who saddle advancement to roll out critical improvement. The best computerized adventures are those that consolidate development with a feeling of direction, whether they are resolving social issues, propelling manageability objectives, or just working on individuals' personal satisfaction.

In this fragment, we'll dive into impact driven business. We'll examine how perceiving social necessities and using development to address them can not solely be a wellspring of fulfillment yet likewise a fundamental method for managing building areas of strength for a successful modernized business.

Exploring the Administrative Scene The administrative climate that oversees the advanced scene evolves with it. Any digital entrepreneur must have a solid understanding of the legal and regulatory landscape in order to reduce risks and ensure compliance. From data security guidelines to safeguarded development considerations, investigating the managerial domain requires a proactive strategy.

This section will give a framework of key genuine examinations in the high level space. Whether you're shipping off a startup, developing worldwide, or partaking in cross-line trades, understanding the regulatory nuances will support your business against conceivable genuine challenges.

Conclusion: Charting Your Course

As we wrap up this examination of the high level scene, it's key to see that understanding the scene is just the most essential stage in your journey. Equipped with data about the headway of electronic wealth, most recent things, and the different entryways open, you're as of now ready to outline your course through the huge high level scene. The following parts will furnish you with the viewpoint, procedures, and suitable devices expected to change your cognizance into significant stages toward cutting edge accomplishment. In this manner, lock in and prepare to venture to every part of the undeniably exhilarating advanced parkway's exciting bends in the road. Your experience has as of late begun.

Change Your Mind set for Digital Success:

Developing the Demeanor of a Computerized Tycoon

In the consistently developing universe of advanced business, achievement still up in the air by the apparatuses and techniques available to you. Similarly imperative is the outlook you offer of real value. " Mentality Shift for Computerized Achievement" isn't simply a part; it's a groundbreaking excursion into the mental landscape of computerized tycoons. Here, we'll investigate the significant effect of outlook on your capacity to explore difficulties, embrace open doors, and at last cut your way to outcome in the computerized domain.

How to Develop a Millionaire's Mindset

The path to digital success begins within your own head. Developing a tycoon mentality isn't tied in with being brought into the world with a silver spoon or having a particular arrangement of qualities. About embracing a perspective lines up with progress. Computerized moguls share normal mental qualities that have moved them to the levels of accomplishment, and in this segment, we'll disentangle the rules that structure the bedrock of their attitude.

Strength, versatility, and a development situated viewpoint are among the mainstays of a mogul outlook. We'll investigate how to embrace difficulties not as impediments but rather as any open doors for development. Through tales and experiences, you'll find how fruitful computerized business people approach misfortunes with a mentality that powers versatility and steadiness.

Overcoming Mental Blocks

Mental blocks are self-imposed limitations that can impede progress and creativity and frequently stand in the way of digital success. Whether it's apprehension about disappointment, an inability to acknowledge success, or the hesitance to get out of your usual range of familiarity, these psychological barriers can be imposing impediments. In this segment, we'll dig into techniques for distinguishing and destroying these hindrances to open your maximum capacity.

A crucial part of becoming a millionaire mindset is overcoming mental obstacles. The computerized scene remunerates the individuals who hope against hope enormous and act strikingly, and by vanquishing inabilities to think straight, you'll be better prepared to explore the difficulties that come your direction.

Steadiness and Versatility in the Computerized World

In the computerized domain, where change is consistent and challenges are unavoidable, constancy and versatility are important characteristics. Digital millionaires are aware that success is not linear; It's a series of ups and downs and twists and turns. In this part, we'll investigate how to develop the persistence expected to weather conditions storms, gain from disappointments, and continue to push ahead.

Through contextual analyses and useful exhortation, you'll acquire bits of knowledge into the excursions of advanced business visionaries who confronted misfortunes yet arose more grounded. From the beginning of inability to the possible victory, these accounts show the force of perseverance and flexibility despite misfortune. You'll see how failures can be opportunities for development and setbacks can be stepping stones.

Taking on a Pioneer's Outlook

In the high speed universe of computerized business, development isn't an extravagance; it's a need. Taking on a pioneer's attitude implies embracing change, searching out new open doors, and continually developing. We'll investigate how fruitful computerized business visionaries stay on the ball by cultivating a culture of development inside themselves and their groups.

Development isn't restricted to notable innovative progressions; it's additionally about tracking down intelligent fixes to regular difficulties. Whether you're refining your item contributions, streamlining your business processes, or investigating novel showcasing approaches, the trend-setters mentality is a compass that guides you toward consistent improvement.

Adjusting Hazard and Prize

Computerized achievement frequently includes exploring unfamiliar regions and proceeding with carefully weighed out courses of action. Understanding how to adjust chance and prize is a major part of the mogul mentality. In this part, we'll look at the rules that guide fruitful business people in settling on essential choices, from entering new business sectors to putting resources into imaginative advancements.

Risk-taking isn't about total surrender;

It's about making well-thought-out and calculated decisions that advance your company. We'll examine risk relief methodologies and investigate how to embrace vulnerability without surrendering to fear. Toward the finish of this segment, you'll have a nuanced comprehension of chance administration, enabling you to pursue choices that line up with your drawn out vision.

Conclusion: Changing Idea right into it

As we close this investigation of the mentality shift for computerized achievement, recollect that developing a mogul outlook is a continuous excursion, not an objective. The standards talked about in this section are not simple speculations; they are significant methodologies that, when applied reliably, can change your points of view and activities.

In the sections that follow, you'll have the amazing chance to try these mentality standards. From laying out daring objectives to embracing difficulties, each segment will give you commonsense devices to support the mentality shift required for computerized achievement. Thus, lock in and prepare to implant your excursion with the demeanor of a computerized tycoon. The compass that will lead you through the thrilling twilight of the digital landscape is your mindset. The experience is standing by.

Differentiating Advantageous Specialties: Revealing the Arrangement for Cutting edge Flourishing

In the gigantic and consistently broadening modernized business community, accomplishment much of the time relies upon the ability to remove a forte - a specific segment of the market where your expertise, energy, and commitments change perfectly. " Perceiving Gainful Claims to fame" isn't just a section; it's a vital manual for help you with uncovering unseen entryways, grasp customer needs, and position yourself for progress in the serious modernized scene.

Choosing Promising Specialties and Conducting Careful Research

The path to computerized success begins with careful research and a keen eye for anticipated specialties. In this section, we'll jump into the methods of reasoning and devices that can help you with recognizing strengths with the most raised benefit potential. You will gain insights into the craft and study of specialty choice by using watchword analysis and dissecting market patterns.

Getting a handle on the necessities, tendencies, and pain points of your vested party is crucial.

Through context oriented examinations and logical exercises, we'll explore how powerful high level money managers have recognized valuable fortes by changing their inclinations to publicize demand. When you get to the furthest limit of this part, you will have the information to do inside and out research on a specialty and track down potential open doors that meet both your inclinations and your crowd's necessities.

Specialty Market Examination

Recognizing a potential specialty is just the underlying step; the certified charm happens when you lead a broad specialty market assessment. This incorporates evaluating the resistance, sorting out buyer lead, and reviewing the overall reasonableness of the strength. In this segment, we'll tell you the best way to lead a top to bottom examination to ensure the specialty you pick isn't just beneficial yet additionally dependable.

We'll explore gadgets and strategies for merciless assessment, helping you with understanding which isolates productive players in your strength. In addition, we'll analyze the meaning of staying open to promote examples and client lead, ensuring that your specialty stays relevant and well known. Close to the completion of this part, you'll have areas of strength for a point for choosing instructed decisions about the common sense in regards to your picked claim to fame.

Methods for Administering Your Strength

Perceiving a useful specialty is basically the beginning; deciding that specialty is where authentic advancement lies. We'll take a gander at the strategies utilized by computerized business visionaries who have entered worthwhile specialties as well as set up a good foundation for themselves as industry pioneers in this segment. We'll look at the variables that add to specialty strength, including laying out serious areas of strength for a presence and offering excellent benefit.

A crucial component of specialty strength is coming up with an exceptional selling proposition (USP). We'll discuss how to isolate your commitments from rivals, whether through thing progression, unparalleled client help, or key affiliations. By understanding the components of specialty contention, you'll be more ready to arrange your picture as the go-to choice inside your picked market area.

Upgrade inside Your Strength

While overpowering a specialty is an excellent goal, expanding inside that specialty can give additional layers of flexibility and improvement. We'll take a look at the strategies that successful digital entrepreneurs use to build a comprehensive ecosystem that reaches a broader audience, cater to a variety of sub-segments within their niche, and broaden their product or service offerings in this section.

Development isn't just about shipping off new things; it's moreover about exploring different channels, associations, and revenue sources. We'll discuss frameworks for scaling your business inside your strength, whether through thing increases, content upgrade, or geographic expansion. Around the completion of this fragment, you'll have a fundamental diagram for administering your specialty as well as expanding your effect inside it.

Improvement and Change in Specialty Assurance

In the strong universe of automated business, strengths can create, and customer tendencies can move. Business visionaries who succeed perceive the meaning of development and versatility in keeping up with their edge over rivals. In this part, we'll research how to stay ready by endlessly creating inside your claim to fame and changing in accordance with emerging examples.

We'll discuss the occupation of analysis circles, client outlines, and factual studying in leftover delicate to the propelling necessities of your group. Relevant examinations will address how dexterous business visionaries have acclimated to changes in their fortes, ensuring that their commitments stay pertinent and pursued. Around the completion of this section, you'll be furnished with strategies for future-fixing your business inside your picked claim to fame.

Conclusion: Your Claim to fame, Your Domain

As we wrap up our examination of recognizing helpful strengths, remember that your picked specialty is more than a market part; it's the foundation whereupon your automated domain is created. The methods and information discussed in this section provide a framework for selecting a valuable field and thriving in it.

The following parts will develop this foundation, guiding you through the most widely recognized approach to building and scaling your high level business inside your picked claim to fame. As a result, as you get ready to leave on this adventure, keep in mind that your specialty is more than just a niche in the market; it's the material whereupon you'll paint your instance of defeating difficulty in the huge scene of the high level business community. Your domain is pausing; how about we push ahead together.

Building Your Computerized Realm: Making the Underpinnings of Online Achievement

Welcome to the range of potential outcomes, where your vision meets the computerized scene, and the groundwork's of your advanced realm start to come to fruition. " Building Your Computerized Realm" isn't simply a section; it's a plan for changing your yearnings into a vigorous and versatile internet based presence. In this part, we'll explore the mind boggling steps of making a strong field-tested strategy, picking the right plan of action, and laying out a telling computerized presence.

Making a Strong Marketable strategy

At the center of each and every effective computerized domain lies a very much created strategy - a guide that frames your vision, mission, and the essential advances expected to carry your plans to completion. We'll look at the most important parts of a digital-focused business plan in this section.

We'll walk you through the steps that will shape the direction of your digital empire, from defining your unique value proposition to conducting a comprehensive market analysis. Contextual analyses and reasonable activities will show how effective business visionaries have utilized marketable strategies to explore difficulties, secure subsidizing, and remain fixed on their drawn out targets.

Picking the Right Plan of action

The computerized scene offers a horde of plans of action, each with its own assets and contemplations.

Picking the right plan of action is a basic choice that will influence your income streams, versatility, and generally maintainability. In this segment, we'll investigate well known advanced plans of action, from web based business and membership administrations to subsidiary advertising and computerized items.

Understanding the subtleties of every plan of action is fundamental for adjusting your contributions to advertise request. We'll examine how effective computerized business visionaries have picked and adjusted their plans of action in light of industry patterns and shopper inclinations

Setting Up Your Advanced Presence

In the advanced age, your web-based presence is the doorway to your realm. This part is your manual for laying out a convincing and legitimate computerized presence that reverberates with your interest group. We'll dig into the complexities of making an expert site, improving your web-based entertainment profiles, and using other computerized channels to upgrade your deceivability.

From making drawing in satisfied to executing compelling Website optimization procedures, you'll figure out how to boost your web-based deceivability and draw in your optimal crowd. Contextual investigations will feature the development of computerized brands and the job serious areas of strength for a presence play in building trust and validity. At the end of this section, you will have the tools you need to start and keep growing your digital presence.

Building a Brand that Resounds

Your image is the heartbeat of your computerized realm - it imparts your qualities, lays out trust, and recognizes you from contenders. In this segment, we'll investigate the components of building a brand that reverberates with your main interest group. From planning an essential logo to creating a convincing brand story, we'll direct you through the means that add to a strong brand character.

Contextual analyses of effective computerized brands will show how vital marking plays had a critical impact in their development. Whether you're a solopreneur or driving a group, understanding the standards of compelling marking will establish the vibe for how your computerized domain is seen on the lookout.

Utilizing Innovation for Productivity

Innovation is the foundation of any advanced realm. In this segment, we'll investigate how to use the most recent devices and stages to smooth out your tasks, upgrade efficiency, and remain in front of the opposition. We'll walk you through the technology landscape that can improve your business efficiency, from collaboration and project management tools to automation and analytics.

The essential reconciliation of innovation saves time as well as positions your computerized domain for adaptability. We'll examine the significance of remaining informed about arising advances and how effective business visionaries have embraced development to impel their organizations forward.

Guaranteeing online protection and Security

With the huge open doors introduced by the computerized scene come likely dangers, particularly in the domains of online protection and security. This segment will dig into the significance of shielding your computerized domain against digital dangers and guaranteeing the protection of your clients and clients.

We'll investigate best practices for online protection, from secure site conventions to information encryption. Understanding the standards of protection and security safeguards your business as well as fabricates entrust with your crowd. You can learn how to build a robust digital fortress for your empire from case studies of businesses that have overcome cyber security challenges successfully.

Conclusion: From Vision to The real world

As we finish up the investigation of building your computerized domain, recall that each example of overcoming adversity starts with a dream and is acknowledged through essential preparation and execution. The resulting parts will dive further into the techniques and strategies expected to scale your domain, yet the establishments laid here are your take off platform.

Your computerized realm is something other than a business; it's an indication of your fantasies and goals. Thus, as you leave on this excursion, imagine the levels you try to reach and the effect you intend to make. Your computerized domain isn't simply an objective; it's a dynamic and steadily developing experience. Let's sail into the infinite potential horizon, where your vision becomes a reality.

Success through Social Media: Becoming amazing at Advanced Impact

In the time of network, web-based entertainment has arisen as a force to be reckoned with, changing the manner in which people and organizations cooperate with the world. " Utilizing Web-based Entertainment for Progress" is something other than a section; it's your manual for becoming the best at advanced impact. In this part, we'll unwind the systems, strategies, and best practices that can lift your image, draw in your crowd, and push your computerized accomplishment through the unique domain of online entertainment.

Web-based Entertainment Promoting Techniques

Your excursion into web-based entertainment achievement starts with a complete comprehension of viable showcasing methodologies. In this part, we'll investigate how to make a web-based entertainment promoting plan that lines up with your business objectives. From distinguishing your main interest group to choosing the right stages and creating convincing substance, you'll acquire bits of knowledge into the key parts that drive effective online entertainment crusades.

Assembling and Connecting with Your Crowd

In the packed computerized field, constructing a dedicated and connected with crowd is the foundation of online entertainment achievement. We'll dig into the techniques that fruitful forces to be reckoned with and brands use to really develop their supporters. From utilizing client created content to encouraging significant cooperation's, you'll figure out how to transform your virtual entertainment presence into a flourishing local area.

Understanding the subtleties of every web-based entertainment stage is urgent for fitting your substance to resound with your crowd. We'll talk about how to advance your profile, curate drawing in posts, and use elements, for example, stories and live video to associate with your supporters. Toward the finish of this part, you'll be outfitted with the information to draw in as well as hold a crowd of people that advocate your image.

Augmenting Virtual Entertainment Stages

The virtual entertainment scene is different, with every stage offering remarkable open doors for commitment. In this part, we'll investigate the significant virtual entertainment stages - from Facebook and Instagram to Twitter, LinkedIn, and arising stages - and talk about systems for amplifying your effect on each.

Whether you're a visual narrator utilizing Instagram's visual allure or an expert interfacing with industry peers on LinkedIn, we'll give bits of knowledge into fitting your methodology for various stages. The art of cross-platform synergy will be demonstrated through case studies of brands that have achieved success across multiple platforms.

Content Creation and Curation

Convincing substance is the backbone of web-based entertainment achievement. In this part, we'll investigate the standards of powerful happy creation and curation. From making eye catching visuals to composing drawing in subtitles, you'll figure out how to make content that reverberates with your crowd as well as urges them to share and lock in.

We'll talk about the significance of authenticity and storytelling in humanizing your brand. Contextual investigations of fruitful web-based entertainment missions will exhibit the variety of content techniques that stand out enough to be noticed of millions. Whether you're making pictures, recordings, or composed content, you'll find how to tailor your way to deal with charm your crowd and pass on your image message actually.

Force to be reckoned with Promoting and Organizations

Cooperation is a strong impetus for virtual entertainment achievement. In this segment, we'll investigate the universe of powerhouse advertising and associations. From distinguishing expected colleagues to organizing commonly valuable associations, you'll acquire bits of knowledge into utilizing the span and impact of others to intensify your image.

Contextual analyses of effective powerhouse joint efforts will grandstand the effect of vital associations. You will learn the art of forging connections that drive engagement and growth, whether you are a brand looking to reach a broader audience or a micro-influencer looking to collaborate with like-minded individuals.

Analytics and Performance Measuring In the ever-evolving social media environment, data serves as your compass. In this segment, we'll investigate the apparatuses and measurements that assist you with estimating the exhibition of your virtual entertainment endeavors. From following commitment measurements to investigating transformation rates, you'll acquire experiences into the key presentation pointers (KPIs) that make the biggest difference for your business.

Understanding investigation not just gives a depiction of your ongoing presentation yet additionally directs future methodologies. We'll talk about how fruitful brands use information to refine their virtual entertainment approach and adjust to evolving patterns. Whether you're centered around brand mindfulness, commitment, or changes, you'll figure out how to decipher information to drive informed navigation.

Adjusting to Calculation Changes and Patterns

The virtual entertainment scene is dynamic, with calculations and patterns continually advancing. In this segment, we'll investigate how to remain on the ball by adjusting to changes in calculations and utilizing arising patterns. From dominating algorithmic courses of events to embracing new elements and configurations, you'll figure out how to situate your image at the front of virtual entertainment development.

Contextual analyses of organizations that have effectively adjusted to calculation changes and outfit arising patterns will give experiences into the deftness required for supported achievement. Whether it's the ascent of short-structure video content or the joining of expanded reality, you'll find how to explore the consistently changing scene of online entertainment.

Conclusion: Enabling Your Computerized Impact

As we finish up our investigation of utilizing virtual entertainment for progress, recall that advanced impact isn't just about numbers; it's tied in with building significant associations and having an enduring effect. The ensuing sections will dig further into explicit methodologies for scaling your computerized impact, yet the standards talked about here are your establishment.

Your excursion into the domain of web-based entertainment achievement isn't a run; a long distance race requires consistency, inventiveness, and a veritable association with your crowd. Thus, as you set out on this intriguing experience, recollect that your computerized impact is an impression of your credibility and the worth you bring to the advanced scene. We should enhance your voice, connect with your crowd, and specialty a story that reverberates across the online entertainment circle. Your impact anticipates - how about we make it unprecedented.

Strategies for Earning Money: Enhancing Revenue Streams for Computerized Flourishing

In the dynamic embroidery of the computerized scene, adaptation is the craft of transforming enthusiasm and development into practical income streams. " More than just a chapter, "Monetization Strategies" it's your manual for exploring the different roads of computerized pay. In this segment, we'll investigate systems for broadening your income streams, opening the capability of automated revenue, and scaling your monetary progress in the powerful universe of online business venture.

Expanding Revenue Sources

The groundwork of a versatile computerized business lies in the variety of its revenue sources. Strategies for reducing reliance on a single revenue stream, diversifying your revenue sources, and creating a more robust and long-lasting financial model will be discussed in this section.

From partner advertising and supported content to item deals and membership administrations, we'll investigate the large number of ways effective computerized business visionaries adapt their endeavors. Contextual analyses will outline how expansion improves your monetary solidness as well as opens new roads for development and advancement.

Opportunities for Passive Income

The ability to generate income with little ongoing effort is what draws people to passive income. In this part, we'll investigate the idea of automated revenue and disclose techniques for integrating it into your advanced plan of action. From subsidiary advertising and computerized items to ventures and sovereignties, you'll find how to make floods of pay that work for you, even while you rest.

Understanding the standards of recurring, automated revenue permits you to construct a business that rises above the limitations of overall setting. We'll examine how fruitful computerized business people influence mechanization, designation, and innovation to open the maximum capacity of recurring, automated revenue valuable open doors.

Scaling Your Income

Scaling your income isn't just about expanding the numbers; It involves developing systems that enable your company to expand at an exponential rate. We'll look at ways to grow your digital business, from improving your sales funnel to adding more products or services, in this section.

We'll talk about how scalability is crucial to creating a profitable and long-lasting business. Contextual analyses of organizations that have effectively scaled their income will delineate the standards of key development. Whether you're a solopreneur or driving a group, you'll acquire bits of knowledge into the versatility methodologies that line up with your business objectives.

Broadening through Numerous Stages

The computerized scene gives a huge number of stages to contacting your crowd and adapting your substance. In this part, we'll investigate how effective business people broaden their pay by utilizing different stages. From web based business commercial centers and virtual entertainment to podcasting and video web based, you'll figure out how to decisively utilize various stages to grow your span and income potential.

The nuances of diversification can be gleaned from case studies of individuals and brands who have successfully accessed multiple platforms. Whether you're a substance maker, web based business person, or specialist co-op, understanding the cooperative energy between stages is vital to expanding your adaptation endeavors.

Making and Selling Advanced Items

Computerized items address a strong road for adaptation, permitting you to change your mastery and inventiveness into substantial resources. In this part, we'll investigate the most common way of making and selling advanced items, from digital books and online courses to programming and computerized downloads.

We'll examine the means engaged with ideation, creation, and showcasing of computerized items. The potential of this monetization strategy will be demonstrated by case studies of people whose digital product sales have resulted in successful businesses. Whether you're an instructor, craftsman, or tech lover, making and selling computerized items can turn into a foundation of your income model.

Membership and Participation Models

Membership and participation models offer a repetitive income stream, encouraging a steady and unsurprising pay for your computerized business. Whether you're offering premium content, exclusive services, or community access, we'll look at how to implement subscription and membership models in this section.

We'll examine the advantages of cultivating a dedicated supporter or part base and how to make esteem that empowers progressing commitment. Contextual investigations of effective membership based organizations will give experiences into the systems and strategies that add to long haul adaptation achievement.

We'll talk about how to pick the right member associations, successfully advance items, and upgrade your subsidiary promoting technique for most extreme returns. Contextual analyses of fruitful associate advertisers will grandstand the variety of approaches inside this adaptation model.

Putting resources into Your Monetary Future

Past the immediate adaptation of your computerized business, key monetary preparation and speculation can add to long haul establishing a strong financial foundation. In this segment, we'll investigate how effective business people approach money management, whether in stocks, land, or different vehicles.

Understanding the standards of monetary administration and

speculation permits you to make an economical and strong monetary future. We'll examine the significance of expanding your ventures and adjusting hazard to construct a strong monetary portfolio.

Conclusion: Adapting with Reason

As we close our investigation of adaptation methodologies, recollect that the best advanced organizations are not exclusively centered around income but rather likewise on making worth and effect. The ensuing parts will dive further into explicit systems for enhancing your adaptation endeavors, yet the standards examined here are your establishment.

Your excursion into the universe of adaptation isn't just about bringing in cash; about building a business lines up with your qualities, serves your crowd, and adds to your drawn out monetary achievement. Thus, as you leave on this thrilling endeavor, imagine the effect you intend to make and the inheritance you seek to make. Let's diversify with intention, monetize with purpose, and create a financial future that reflects your contribution to the digital landscape. Your computerized thriving anticipates - we should make it remarkable.

Money related arrangement and Flood the bosses: Exploring the Way to Independence from a pointless everyday presence

In the phenomenal scene of robotized undertaking, making and controlling financial thriving isn't just about conveying pay; It is connected to creating a financially secure and dependable future. Financial planning and Overflow "The board" is more than just a part of; it's your manual for examining the intricacies of speculation, making heads or tails of the standards of flood the bosses, and cultivating a perspective that prompts independence from the purposeless everyday presence in the modernized age.

Figuring out Experience Basics

Contributing is a supporting of flood creation, and understanding its fundamentals is essential for bringing in informed cash related choices. In this part, we'll investigate the fundamentals of strong financial planning, from various resource classes like stocks and securities to the standards of risk and return.

We will discuss the key ideas that structure the support of compelling endeavor frameworks, whether you are just starting out or a meticulously planned financial donor. We'll talk about what "widening" means, how to stop risk, and what reasonable financial goals are. Sensible encounters into the universe of cash the executives can be assembled from relevant examinations of people whose overflow was dealt with fundamental endeavors.

Procedures for Building an Undertaking Portfolio

Developing significant areas of fortitude for a portfolio requires a crucial system that lines up with your monetary objectives and hazard flexibility. In this piece, we'll jump into different undertaking strategies, from moderate approaches to overseeing extra strong ones, and take a gander at how to oblige your portfolio to your striking conditions.

We'll talk about portfolio rebalancing, asset allocation, and how your investment strategy is affected by your time horizon. Setting focused assessments of convincing money related allies will approach the scope of portfolio improvement and the importance of adjusting to changing monetary conditions.

Researching the Insurances exchange

The insurances exchange, with its hazards and doorways, is a focal field for flood creation. We'll take a gander at how to investigate the protections trade in this part, covering points like stock basics, market examples, and going with taught venture choices.

We'll discuss the methodologies that turn out best for your venture goals, whether you like to exchange traded holds (ETFs) or normal resources or individual stocks. Monetary supporters who have effectively investigated the intricacies of the protections trade will be highlighted in certifiable models and context oriented examinations.

Techniques for Land Hypothesis Land is a huge and reliable method for laying out monetary security. In this segment, we will look at different land venture methodologies, including fix-and-flip organizations, investment properties, and land speculation trusts (REITs). We'll dissect the standards of property valuation, funding, and risk the board.

The different points of view one can take on the land hypothesis scene can be acquired from logical investigations of fruitful land lenders. Whether you are an accomplished financial backer hoping to extend your portfolio or a first-time homebuyer seeking influence land for abundance creation, you will acquire significant points of view on land speculation.

Understanding Cryptographic money and Elective Undertakings

The ascending of automated resources, including modernized money related guidelines, has added another viewpoint to the undertaking scene. In this part, we'll look at the universe of cryptographic money and elective speculations, talking about the doorways and dangers related with these driving resources.

We'll talk about the fundamentals of block chain technology, how to put money into cryptographic forms, and how to remember computerized resources for your overall growth strategy. Pieces of information into the influential thought of this emerging hypothesis class will be given by relevant examinations of monetary supporters who have actually investigated the computerized currency market.

Key Retirement Orchestrating Imperative retirement organizing goes past basically committing to a retirement account. Making game plans for retirement is a central piece of overflow the leaders. We will investigate retirement orchestrating strategies in this section, including individual retirement accounts (IRAs), business-sponsored plans, and other retirement vehicles.

We'll talk about the standards of evaluation arranging, withdrawal methodologies, and the control of Government retirement assistant in retirement pay. Setting focused assessments of people who have indisputably expected retirement will show the significance of a wide and vital strategy for overseeing retirement save holds.

Risk Management and Overflow Insurance Saving and protecting your overflow is just as important as building it. Frameworks for risk the board and overflow preservation, for instance, security, space organizing, and asset confirmation, will be analyzed in this section.

Understanding how to explore the intricacies of domain sorting out, limit charge liabilities, and shield your resources from surprising risks is fundamental for making a helping through monetary heritage. Relevant studies of people who have successfully saved and protected their excess will provide useful insights into the principles of excess.

Making an Independence from the vain everyday presence Outlook

Past the particular bits of reasonable financial readiness and flood the board, encouraging an independence from a purposeless day to day presence mentality is the best way to deal with significant length achievement. We'll look at how demeanor and mind science contribute to financial success in this section.

We'll examine that it is so fundamental to learn about cash, set forth targets, and manage your overflow in a controlled way. Legitimate records of people who have vanquished cash related difficulties and accomplished independence from a vain lifestyle will invigorate and give crucial methods to empowering a point of view that prompts traversing thriving.

Persevering Learning and Assortment

The universe of money and experience is dynamic, with financial conditions and financial scenes incessantly making. In this part, we'll underline the significance of tireless learning and change in the space of convincing money related readiness and flood the board.

We'll examine assets for remaining instructed, the control of mentorship, and how strong financial supporters and spill over managers adjust to propelling conditions. Understanding the worth of well established learning is fundamental for upheld progress in the continually impacting universe of cash, whether you are a beginner monetary supporter or an accomplished monetary master.

Conclusion: Your Way to Independence from a pointless day to day presence

As we wrap up our assessment of strong money the chiefs and flood the board, recall that your excursion to independence from the purposeless day to day presence is extraordinary and different. Although the guidelines discussed here form the foundation of your financial journey, the following sections will go into greater detail about clear methods and procedures for working on your project.

Your way to independence from a worthless lifestyle isn't just about storing flood; It's connected to making a presence of security, reason, and flood. Likewise, as you set out on this totally thrilling endeavor, imagine the way of life you expect, the effect you wish to make, and the inheritance you mean to leave. Together, we should investigate the path to financial freedom, where abundance is a dynamic and enabling journey rather than merely a goal. Your monetary future expects - might we at any point make it remarkable.

Computerization and Scaling: Organizing Productivity for Advanced Development

Welcome to the domain where productivity meets outstanding development - "Mechanization and Scaling." This isn't simply a section; it's your manual for releasing the force of robotization, enhancing cycles, and scaling your computerized tries higher than ever. In this segment, we'll investigate systems, devices, and rules that enable you to robotize dull errands, smooth out work processes, and scale your tasks for supported progress in the unique advanced scene.

The Specialty of Mechanization

Mechanization is the impetus that pushes advanced organizations past the requirements of time and assets. In this part, we'll dig into the specialty of mechanization, investigating how to recognize undertakings ready for robotization and executing apparatuses and advancements that smooth out your work processes.

We'll examine the standards of work process examination, the job of robotization in upgrading efficiency, and genuine instances of organizations that have embraced computerization to accomplish functional productivity. Whether you're a solopreneur or driving a group, understanding the basics of mechanization makes way for versatile development.

Implementing Efficient Systems A scalable digital operation is built on efficient systems. In this segment, we'll investigate how to plan and carry out frameworks that improve productivity, decrease bottlenecks, and make an establishment for consistent scaling.

From project the board and specialized devices to client relationship the executives (CRM) frameworks, we'll talk about the key parts that add to proficient tasks. Contextual investigations of organizations that have effectively carried out productive frameworks will show the groundbreaking effect of all around planned processes.

Scaling Your Computerized Framework

Scaling isn't just about filling in size; it's tied in with extending your advanced framework to oblige expanded requests. In this segment, we'll investigate techniques for scaling your advanced framework, from distributed computing and server improvement to content conveyance organizations (CDNs) and load adjusting.

Understanding the standards of adaptability permits your advanced business to deal with development without compromising execution. We'll examine how fruitful organizations have explored the difficulties of scaling their advanced foundation and offer bits of knowledge into arriving at informed conclusions about innovation ventures.

Internet business Scaling Procedures

For internet business people, scaling includes expanding deals as well as advancing the whole client venture. In this segment, we'll investigate web based business scaling techniques, from improving site execution to carrying out proficient request satisfaction and client service frameworks.

We'll examine how to use innovation to deal with expanded traffic, enhance the checkout interaction, and customize the shopping experience. Contextual analyses of internet business organizations that have effectively scaled their tasks will give noteworthy experiences to those hoping to extend their web-based adventures.

Showcasing Mechanization for Development

Promoting is a critical component of computerized development, and robotization is the key part that empowers customized and versatile showcasing endeavors. In this segment, we'll investigate showcasing mechanization methodologies, from email promoting and lead sustaining to web-based entertainment computerization and information driven direction.

Understanding the standards of advertising computerization permits you to draw in with your crowd at scale without forfeiting personalization. We'll examine how fruitful advertisers use robotization to smooth out their missions, support leads, and measure the adequacy of their techniques.

Scaling Content Creation and Conveyance

Content is the backbone of computerized commitment, and scaling content creation and dispersion is a critical driver of development. From using content creation tools and creating a content calendar to optimizing distribution across multiple channels, we'll look at scaling your content efforts in this section.

We'll talk about the significance of reusing content, teaming up with content makers, and utilizing investigation to refine your substance methodology. Insights into the various approaches to content creation and distribution can be gained from case studies of businesses that have scaled their content operations successfully.

Robotizing Client service and Commitment

Client service is a basic part of computerized achievement, and computerization can upgrade the productivity of your help tasks. From self-service options and knowledge bases to chatbots and automated responses, we'll look at ways to automate customer support and engagement in this section.

We'll examine how mechanization can further develop reaction times, give day in and day out help, and upgrade the general client experience. Contextual analyses of organizations that have effectively carried out mechanized client service frameworks will exhibit the advantages of utilizing innovation in client commitment.

Monetary Computerization for Business Effectiveness

Monetary administration is a center part of maintaining a computerized business, and computerization can smooth out monetary cycles for expanded effectiveness. In this segment, we'll investigate monetary robotization systems, from invoicing and cost following to finance and bookkeeping.

Not only does it save time to learn how to automate financial workflows, but it also lowers the likelihood of making mistakes and ensures compliance. We'll examine the standards of monetary robotization and offer experiences from organizations that have enhanced their monetary cycles for effectiveness and exactness.

Ceaseless Streamlining and Transformation

In the high speed computerized scene, ceaseless advancement is the way to remaining on the ball. In this part, we'll investigate the standards of constant streamlining and variation, from examining information and social occasion criticism to refining cycles and embracing arising advancements.

We'll examine the significance of a culture of trial and error and realizing, where groups are urged to repeat and improve constantly. Contextual investigations of organizations that have effectively embraced a mentality of ceaseless streamlining will give viable bits of knowledge to those hoping to cultivate a culture of development.

Conclusion: Coordinating Your Computerized Ensemble

As we close our investigation of computerization and scaling, recall that it's not just about accomplishing more; it's tied in with doing all the more effectively. The resulting parts will dig further into explicit procedures and strategies for advancing your robotization endeavors, however the standards talked about here are the groundwork of your computerized orchestra.

Your journey into the world of scaling and automation involves more than just streamlining procedures; about organizing an ensemble of productivity resounds all through your computerized business. Thus, as you leave on this intriguing endeavor, imagine the agreeable mix of innovation and methodology that pushes your business higher than ever. We should mechanize with accuracy, scale with aim, and make a computerized orchestra that reverberations achievement. Your arranged development anticipates - we should make it remarkable.

Overcoming Obstacles and Mistakes: Welcome to "Overcoming Challenges and Failures," the chapter in which setbacks are viewed as stepping stones rather than obstacles.

This isn't simply a section; it's your manual for exploring the inescapable obstacles on your excursion to computerized achievement, changing misfortune into flexibility, and involving disappointments as impetuses for development. In this segment, we'll investigate methodologies, outlook movements, and certifiable models that enable you to defeat difficulties and arise more grounded on the way to progress.

Developing a Growth Mindset Cultivating a growth mindset—the belief that intelligence and abilities can be developed through dedication and hard work—is the foundation for overcoming obstacles. In this part, we'll dig into the standards of a development mentality and investigate how taking on this point of view can enable you to explore difficulties with versatility and an emphasis on learning.

We'll examine the significance of rethinking disappointments as any open doors for development and offer experiences from people who have embraced the development attitude to conquer affliction. Whether you're confronting misfortunes in your profession, business, or individual life, understanding and developing a development outlook is the most important move towards beating difficulties.

The Value of Failure The Force of Versatility

Disappointment isn't the end; it's a turn point for development. In this part, we'll investigate the force of flexibility and how to transform disappointments into significant examples. We'll talk about how to use adversity as a springboard for personal and professional growth, reframe failures as opportunities, and how to bounce back from setbacks.

Genuine instances of people who have confronted and beaten disappointments will give motivation and commonsense bits of knowledge into building strength. Whether it's an undertaking that didn't take off or a task that didn't go as expected, flexibility is the way to exploring the erratic idea of the computerized scene.

Methodologies for Critical thinking

Challenges are innate in any undertaking, however powerful critical thinking methodologies can transform hindrances into wins. In this segment, we'll investigate critical thinking systems, from distinguishing main drivers to carrying out arrangements and estimating results.

We'll talk about how fruitful people and organizations approach critical thinking,	underlining	the significance	of	joint	effort, innovativeness,	and	versatility. Contextual analyses of associations that	have	explored	complex difficulties through essential critical thinking	will	give	viable experiences	to	handling impediments	in	your	own computerized venture.

Building an Emotionally supportive network

Confronting difficulties alone can be overwhelming, and that is the reason fabricating an emotionally supportive network is essential for conquering snags. We will discuss the significance of mentorship, networking, and being surrounded by a supportive community in this section.

We'll talk about how looking for counsel and direction from tutors can give important viewpoints and bits of knowledge. The impact of community and collaboration on the path to success will be demonstrated by case studies of people who have overcome obstacles by utilizing their support networks.

Overseeing Pressure and Burnout

The computerized scene can be requesting, and overseeing pressure and burnout is fundamental for long haul achievement. In this segment, we'll investigate procedures for keeping up with mental and profound prosperity, from rehearsing care and defining limits to perceiving the indications of burnout and looking for proficient help.

We'll talk about the significance of taking care of oneself and offer experiences from people who have focused on their prosperity in the midst of the difficulties of the advanced world. Whether you're a business person, consultant, or some portion of a bigger association, understanding how to oversee pressure and forestall burnout is significant for supported achievement.

Adjusting to Change and Vulnerability

The main steady in the computerized scene is change, and figuring out how to adjust is a vital expertise for beating difficulties. We'll look at ways to deal with change and uncertainty in this section, from cultivating a flexible mindset to learning how to be adaptable.

We'll talk about how fruitful people and organizations embrace change as a chance for development and advancement. Practical tips for navigating the digital world's unpredictable nature can be found in case studies of businesses that have successfully adapted to shifts in the industry and market.

Converting Setbacks into Opportunities Failures are not defeats; they're potential open doors for rebounds. In this segment, we'll investigate the specialty of transforming misfortunes into rebounds, from dissecting disappointments and gaining from errors to recapturing force and rethinking achievement.

We'll examine how strength, determination, and an essential outlook can change difficulties into venturing stones towards more prominent accomplishments. For your own digital journey, real-world examples of people who have overcome obstacles and orchestrated successful comebacks will inspire you and provide you with actionable strategies.

Looking for and Embracing Criticism

Criticism is an amazing asset for development, and looking for and embracing input is a vital part of beating difficulties. In this segment, we'll investigate the standards of input, from effectively looking for contribution to involving valuable analysis as an impetus for development.

We'll talk about how having a mindset that values feedback can help you keep getting better and be resilient in the face of challenges. Practical insights into the transformative power of constructive input will be provided by case studies of individuals and organizations that have utilized feedback to overcome obstacles and achieve success.

Observing Little Wins and Achievements

In the midst of difficulties, celebrating little wins and achievements is a vital part of keeping up with inspiration and force. In this segment, we'll investigate the brain research of accomplishment, from laying out sensible objectives to perceiving and celebrating progress en route.

We'll examine how recognizing little wins adds to a positive mentality and makes an establishment for conquering bigger difficulties. Contextual investigations of people and organizations that have embraced the act of commending achievements will give motivation to integrating this technique into your own advanced excursion.

Conclusion: Your Excursion of Win

As we finish up our investigation of beating difficulties and disappointments, recall that misfortunes are not the finish of the excursion; they're potential open doors for development and change. The ensuing sections will dive further into explicit techniques for flexibility and achievement, yet the standards examined here are your establishment.

Your excursion in the advanced scene isn't characterized.

Contextual investigations of Advanced Moguls: Moving Excursions to Abundance and Achievement

In this part, we will dig into the rousing accounts of people who have explored the computerized scene, defeat difficulties, and accomplished the sought after status of advanced moguls. These contextual analyses act as windows into different ways to progress, giving bits of knowledge, examples, and inspiration for those trying to cut their own ways in the powerful universe of online business venture.

1st Case Study: The Exploring Business person

Name: Sarah Chang

Foundation:

Sarah Chang, a former executive, set out on her entrepreneurial journey motivated by a desire to live sustainably. Perceiving the rising interest for eco-accommodating items, she established an online business stage represent considerable authority in maintainable and moral way of life items.

Key Achievement Variables:

Expertise in a Specific Field: Sarah utilized her energy and skill in practical living, taking care of a developing business sector looking for naturally cognizant items.

Web based business Development: She embraced the force of online business, using easy to understand stages, and carrying out proficient inventory network and satisfaction frameworks.

Content Advertising: Sarah created a community around her brand by educating and engaging her audience about sustainable living through content marketing techniques like blogging and social media.

Scaling Manageability: As attention to maintainability developed, Sarah extended her product offering, teamed up with powerhouses, and decisively entered worldwide business sectors, scaling her business universally.

Name: Alex Rodriguez

Foundation:

Alex Rodriguez started out as a content creator on a well-known platform for sharing videos. He started out making entertaining videos and gradually moved on to making educational content about investing and personal finance.

Key Achievement Elements:

Validness and Appeal: Alex's credibility and appeal drew an enormous and committed crowd. He straightforwardly shared his monetary excursion, making complex themes available to his watchers.

Diversification: Past promotion income, Alex broadened his revenue streams by sending off web-based courses, composing a smash hit book, and participating in member showcasing organizations.

Local area Building: Perceiving the force of local area, Alex effectively drew in with his crowd through live meetings, back and forth discussions, and elite substance, cultivating a feeling of having a place among his devotees.

Adaptability: To stay ahead of the curve, Alex modified his content to address emerging trends like crypto currency and alternative investments as the financial landscape changed.

Contextual investigation 3: The Tech Trend-setter

Name: Maya Patel

Foundation:

Maya Patel, a tech lover, established a startup zeroed in on creating state of the art man-made consciousness (artificial intelligence) answers for organizations. Her process included exploring the tech business' difficulties and situating her organization as a forerunner in simulated intelligence development.

Key Achievement Variables:

Innovation: Maya's organization was at the cutting edge of computer based intelligence advancement, creating arrangements that tended to true business challenges. This obligation to development put her aside in a serious market.

Key Associations: Maya manufactured key organizations with industry pioneers, empowering her startup to get to assets, skill, and a more extensive client base.

Recruiting new talent: Perceiving the significance of a gifted group, Maya zeroed in on enrolling top ability in the computer based intelligence field. Her group's skill assumed a critical part in the organization's prosperity.

Solutions that Can Grow: The arrangements Maya's organization created were intended for versatility, permitting them to serve both private companies and huge undertakings. This adaptability added to quick development.

Contextual investigation 4: The Advanced Financial backer

Name: Jason Wang

Foundation:

Jason Wang started his profession as a computerized financial backer, zeroing in on digital currency and blockchain innovation. Beginning with unassuming ventures, he decisively explored the unpredictable crypto market to create significant financial wellbeing.

Key Achievement Variables:

Instructive Venture: Jason committed opportunity to teach himself about the complexities of cryptographic money and blockchain, pursuing informed venture choices.

Management of risk: Perceiving the instability of the crypto market, Jason carried out risk the board methodologies, enhancing his portfolio and remaining refreshed on market patterns.

Long haul Viewpoint: Instead of capitulating to momentary market vacillations, Jason kept a drawn out point of view, enduring business sector slumps and exploiting the business' general development.

Local area Commitment: Jason effectively drew in with the digital money local area, taking part in discussions, going to gatherings, and remaining associated with industry specialists. This systems administration gave significant experiences and open doors.

Contextual analysis 5: The Online business Dissident

Name: Olivia Bennett

Foundation:

Olivia Bennett established a web based business brand gaining practical experience in customized and adaptable items. Her process included distinguishing market patterns, making an exceptional selling recommendation, and using computerized promoting to contact a worldwide crowd.

Key Achievement Variables:

Statistical surveying: Olivia was able to create products that resonated with her target audience because she conducted extensive market research to identify consumer trends and demands.

Personalization and Customization: Separating her image, Olivia zeroed in on offering customized and adaptable items, taking advantage of the developing purchaser inclination for one of a kind and tailor made things.

Advanced Advertising Authority: Utilizing online entertainment publicizing, powerhouse coordinated efforts, and email showcasing, Olivia actually advanced her image, directing people to her web based business stage and creating deals.

Versatility to Patterns: Olivia remained receptive to web based business and configuration patterns, routinely refreshing her item contributions and showcasing procedures to remain pertinent and catch advancing customer interests.

Gaining from Advanced Trailblazers

As we close our investigation of contextual investigations highlighting computerized moguls, recollect that each excursion is special, molded by a blend of development, flexibility, and vital navigation. These accounts offer significant examples and motivation for those exploring their own ways in the always advancing computerized scene.

Whether you reverberate with the online business person, the substance maker turned big shot, the tech trailblazer, the computerized financial backer, or the web based business dissident, the consistent idea among these computerized pioneers is a pledge to nonstop learning, flexibility, and an enthusiasm for what they do. As you set out on your advanced excursion, let these contextual investigations act as signals of motivation, directing you towards your own computerized achievement. Your story is holding on to unfurl - we should make it phenomenal.

Conclusion: Your Excursion to Advanced Success

In this thorough aide, we've left on an extraordinary investigation of the computerized scene, uncovering the methodologies, standards, and moving stories that prepare to computerized flourishing. As you finish up this aide, recall that your excursion in the computerized domain is a dynamic and developing experience, molded by your novel vision, assurance, and eagerness to embrace advancement.

Thinking about Your Advanced Excursion

Pause for a minute to consider the bits of knowledge acquired all through this aide:

Figuring out the Advanced Scene: From the groundwork's of the computerized scene to the complexities of online business, you've acquired a comprehensive perspective on the powerful world in which advanced moguls flourish.

Building Your Advanced Realm: The systems for building a versatile and adaptable computerized domain, from creating a convincing brand to utilizing mechanization and scaling procedures, give a plan to progress.

Adaptation Methodologies: A successful digital business's financial foundation is strengthened by expanding your revenue, exploring passive income opportunities, and diversifying your income streams.

Financial planning and Abundance The board: The foundation for establishing long-term prosperity in the digital age is the ability to navigate the complexities of investing, wealth management, and strategic financial planning.

Robotization and Scaling: Coordinating effectiveness through mechanization and scaling is the way to maintainable development, permitting you to explore the intricacies of a powerful computerized climate.

Conquering Difficulties and Disappointments: Strength, a development outlook, and compelling procedures for beating difficulties change misfortunes into venturing stones toward progress.

Contextual investigations of Advanced Tycoons: Drawing motivation from true contextual investigations, you've seen the different excursions of advanced tycoons, each offering significant illustrations and bits of knowledge.

Embracing Your Computerized Success

As you push ahead on your computerized venture, think about the accompanying standards:

Energy and Reason: Imbue your advanced undertakings with enthusiasm and reason. Adjust your dares to what genuinely moves you, making an establishment for supported inspiration and satisfaction.

Consistent Learning: The digital landscape is changing quickly. Focus on a mentality of ceaseless getting the hang of, remaining informed about arising patterns, innovations, and market elements.

Flexibility and Development: Embrace change and advancement as constants. Be versatile, able to turn, and open to investigating new roads that line up with your objectives.

Local area and Cooperation: Create and maintain a community that is supportive. Find mentorship, work with like-minded people, and contribute to a community of success and growth.

Trustworthiness and Morals: In your digital endeavors, uphold the principles of integrity and ethical behavior. Fabricate entrust with your crowd, clients, and teammates, cultivating long haul connections.

Adaptability in the Face of Obstacles: Challenges are unavoidable; strength is your superpower. Move toward mishaps as any open doors for development, and use disappointments as impetuses for advancement.

Keeping Profit and Purpose in Check: Take a stab at a harmony between monetary achievement and having a constructive outcome. Fabricate an inheritance that reaches out past income, adding to the improvement of society and the world.

Your Advanced Thriving is standing by

As you outline your course in the advanced scene, recall that computerized thriving isn't exclusively estimated in monetary terms; It encompasses a comprehensive vision of success that is in line with your values, goals, and desired impact.

Your process is a material ready to be painted with development, versatility, and reason. Embrace the difficulties, commend the triumphs, and ceaselessly refine your methodologies. Your computerized thriving anticipates - we should make it remarkable. Cheers to your outcome in the dynamic and consistently advancing universe of computerized business venture!